UTAH

A Turner Educational Services, Inc. book. Based on the Portrait
of America television series created by R.E. (Ted) Turner.

Library of Congress Number: 85-12174

4 5 6 7 8 9 10   99 98 97 96 95 94 93 92 91 90

Library of Congress Cataloging in Publication Data

Thompson, Kathleen.
  Utah.

  (Portrait of America)
  "A Turner book."
  Summary: Discusses the history, economy, culture,
and future of Utah. Also includes a state
chronology, pertinent statistics, and maps.
  1. Utah—Juvenile literature. [1. Utah]
I. Title. II. Series: Thompson, Kathleen. Portrait of
America.
F826.3.T46   1985   979.2   85-12174
ISBN 0-86514-446-X (lib. bdg.)
ISBN 0-86514-521-0 (softcover)

Cover Photo: Patrick Dean

★ ★ ★ ★ ★

Portrait of AMERICA

UTAH

Kathleen Thompson

Photographs from Portrait of America programs
courtesy of Turner Program Services, Inc.

A TURNER BOOK
RAINTREE PUBLISHERS

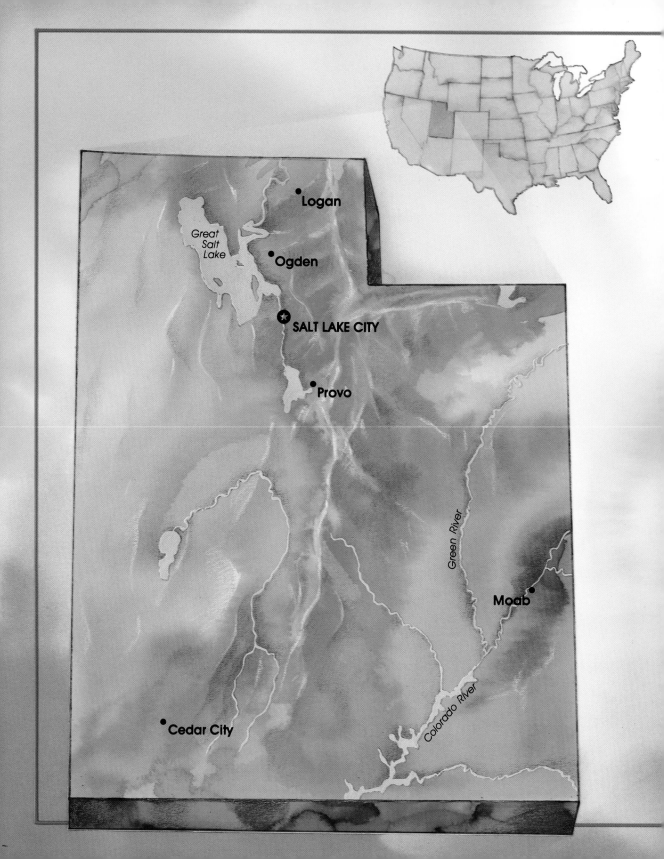

Logan

Great
Salt
Lake

Ogden

★ SALT LAKE CITY

Provo

Green River

Moab

Colorado River

Cedar City

CONTENTS

Introduction

Utah, the Beehive State.

"I don't think there is a country in the world like the United States. This is heaven on earth. And I think Utah is one of the finest states. So, if I could live in the United States and live in Utah, I've got everything."

Utah: Mormons, mines, and the Great Salt Lake, hard ground and hard living.

"If it wasn't hard, I wouldn't want it. . . . A mind and body that isn't struggling . . . isn't worth very much."

Utah was not the first choice of the people who came to live here just over a hundred years ago. It was, in one sense, a last resort. But the people believed it could be a paradise.

That's what made Utah what it is today, a place that has been created as much by the faith and courage of its people as by nature.

The struggle has produced a special kind of community . . . and a special kind of person.

A view from Sunset Point in Bryce Canyon.

This Is the Place

They may have come from Asia during the Ice Age, across the Bering Strait. They were people of the Stone Age and, 10,000 years ago, they lived in caves along the edges of Lake Bonneville.

Then, about A.D. 400, the Anasazi Indians came up from the Southwest. Their advanced culture soon spread through Utah. Their towns were huge apartment buildings. They were good farmers who had developed methods of irrigation. And, like future settlers in Utah, they had a strong religion.

The Anasazi civilization lasted here for over 800 years, almost four times as long as the United States has been a country. And then they disappeared. No one knows exactly

The drawings on the face of this mountain were made by Indians thousands of years ago.

why. It may have been because of a long and terrible drought.

By the time the first Europeans came to Utah, the land was inhabited by the Shoshone, Paiute, Gosiute and Ute tribes. Their desert culture changed when horses were brought to the area. They began to live in larger groups. They hunted buffalo and made their homes in cliffs.

There may have been some Spanish explorers in Utah in the 1500s. But the first Europeans we know about who visited the area were two Roman Catholic priests, Francisco Atanasio Dominguez and Silvestre Velez de Escalante. They were looking for a way to Monterey, California.

The two priests later described the land and its people, but they did not stay. From the time they came in 1776 until the year 1847, there were no European settlers in Utah. Those who came were fur trappers and traders. They were explorers and mountain men. They were men like James Bridger, the first white man to see and describe the Great Salt Lake. Or Jedediah Smith, the first person to travel the state from north to south and east to west. Or Antoine Robidoux, who set up an early trading post on the Green River.

Then, in 1847, the Mormons came. Their settlement was part of a bigger story.

The Church of Jesus Christ of Latter-day Saints was founded in New York in 1830 by Joseph Smith. Almost immediately, groups of church members began to move west, looking for a place where they could practice their religion in peace. They

didn't find it in Kirkland, Ohio. They didn't find it in Independence, Missouri. They didn't find it in Nauvoo, Illinois.

In 1846, the Mormons were forced to leave Nauvoo after Joseph Smith was murdered. This time, under their leader Brigham Young, they were determined to find a place of their own. If necessary, they would take a place no one else wanted. They headed west again. And they came to Utah.

At this time, Utah was part of an area claimed by Mexico. But there were no settlers from any country in Utah when Brigham Young stood near the eastern shore of the Great Salt Lake and said, "This is the place."

More Mormons followed that first small group. Many of them were helped by the Perpetual Emigrating Fund set up by the church in 1849. They came from the eastern United States, from Denmark, Sweden, Norway, and the British Isles.

At the left is a nineteenth-century photograph of Ute Indians. The print below shows Joseph Smith.

In 1848, Utah was given to the United States as part of the treaty that ended the Mexican War.

The Mormons irrigated the land of Utah. They set up farming communities. New colonists were chosen for their skills and abilities. Each settlement was carefully organized to be as self-sufficient as possible. The organization and the discipline were strict, but the Mormon settlements survived in a harsh land.

Two years after their arrival, the settlers organized the "State of Deseret." They drew up a constitution, elected officials, and asked to be admitted to the United States. But it was not that easy. Congress created the Utah Territory but would not make Utah a state. For the next forty-six years, Utah would ask again and again for statehood. Each time it would be refused because of the people's belief in polygamy.

Polygamy is the practice of one man having more than one wife. It was not particularly widespread among Mormons, but it was part of what they believed to be right. For a long time, it was either the reason or the excuse for others to persecute the Mormon community.

At the left is a photograph of Brigham Young against the background of the town of St. George, one of the early Mormon settlements in Utah.

To many people, the Mormons seemed strange. And because they were strange, they seemed dangerous. Also, they were so self-sufficient that non-Mormons had trouble getting a foothold in the territory. Mormons traded with each other. Storekeepers and other businessmen who tried to set up shop in Utah felt as though they were being frozen out.

The Mormons had basically friendly relations with the Indians in the area. Attacks on the settlers in 1853 by a Ute chief named Walker were ended in 1854. Brigham Young convinced him that the Indians and settlers could live together in peace. In 1865, several tribes joined another Ute chief, Black Hawk, in an uprising against the Mormons. Again, talks ended the war.

The Mormons' biggest problems came, not from the Indians, but from other whites.

President James Buchanan, in 1857, heard rumors that Brigham Young—who was then governor of the Utah Territory—was guilty of treason. They were nothing more than rumors, but they gave Buchanan an excuse to try to take Utah away from the Mormons. He appointed a new governor and sent in troops to "quell the rebellion."

As the soldiers marched west towards Utah, the people of Utah waited in fear. Mormons and Indians together attacked a party of travelers that was passing through the state. Most of the 140 people in that party were killed.

The soldiers arrived in 1858 and defeated the people of Utah. They stayed in the state for three years, then left at the beginning of the Civil War. They were followed in 1862 by a group of California volunteers who came to the territory after Congress passed a law against polygamy.

That same law disincorpo-

This is a photograph of U.S. troops that were sent to "quell the rebellion" in Utah in 1858.

rated the Latter-day Saints Church and made it illegal for the church to own more than $50,000 worth of property, not including houses of worship. In 1874, the Poland Act weakened the Mormon court system by establishing federal judges in place of territorial ones. The Edmunds Act of 1882, basically, took away the Mormons' right to vote, put the territory under the control of a government commission, and stiffened the anti-polygamy laws. In 1887, many church lands were taken away.

In 1890, the Mormon church gave in. They did away with polygamy. In 1896, Utah became a state.

The forty-six years from settlement to statehood in Utah were not the federal government's finest hour. Hundreds of Mormons had been fined, persecuted, and put into prison. But there were other things happening in Utah.

From April of 1860 until October of 1861, the pony express traveled across Utah on its way from Missouri to California. It lasted for only a year and a half before it was replaced by the tele-

graph, but it became a part of the legend of the West.

Then there was the great transcontinental railroad. The Central Pacific started building their lines from California east. The Union Pacific started in Nebraska and built west. They met at Promontory, Utah, in 1869. Well, actually, they passed each other there first, but they did manage to get together on May 10 for the Governor of California to hammer in a golden spike. He missed, but the telegraph operator had already sent out the news. New York fired a hundred-gun salute. Philadelphia rang the Liberty Bell. The United States were finally united.

The railroads were very important to Utah. By the turn of the

Kennecott

At the left is a photograph of the meeting of the two parts of the first transcontinental railroad in Promontory in 1869. Above is a copper mine near Salt Lake City.

century, valuable minerals had been found in the state. Mining was an important industry and its products were sent out to the rest of the country on trains. Utah's agricultural products, especially beef cattle and sheep, were shipped on the railroad.

In the early part of the 1900s, factories were built in Utah to process the metals taken from its land. And a huge federal irrigation project opened more farmland.

Then came the Great Depression. The economy of Utah was badly hurt. It began to recover with the rest of the country in the late 1930s. Then World War II brought in the military.

During the war, many war production plants and military bases were built in Utah. The government became the state's biggest employer. Manufacturing became more and more important to Utah's economy. After the war, the military didn't leave. It expanded.

At the same time, more people were moving into all the west-

17

The photograph above is a re-creation of a room in an early Mormon school. The photo below is the Mormon Temple in Salt Lake City. The photo in the background shows the temple and the tabernacle during construction. The temple took forty years to complete, between 1853 and 1893.

ern states. That gave Utah more nearby markets for all their goods. It also brought more people into the state as tourists.

Mormons have always believed in education and that has made the state of Utah a highly educated place. It also caused a problem in the 1960s. Utah's educators insisted that the state needed more than $25 million more in state aid to education. They got

Utah State Historical Society

$11 million. A year later, in 1964, when they asked for $6 million, the governor refused. That caused a crisis.

A national teachers' union, the National Education Association (NEA), called on its members not to take jobs in Utah's schools until the state raised the needed money. It was the first time that such a protest had been raised against a whole state.

The legislature found the money for education and the NEA boycott was called off. Today, the people of Utah average more years in school than people in any other state. And Utah spends a larger part of its income for schools than most other states.

The story of Utah has, clearly, been closely tied to the Church of Jesus Christ of Latter-day Saints. About three quarters of Utah's population is Mormon. But, since 1936, the church has been officially neutral in politics. Several non-Mormons have served as governor of the state.

Still, the Mormons have made Utah's history unique. They are a large part of what happens in the fascinating state.

The Mormon Majority

"One of the feelings you have about being a Mormon, and that is, you're a member of a church that is a Christian church and yet vastly different from others, to the extent where they look at you and say, 'Well, you're not a Christian church because you're so different than we are.' And my usual response to that is, 'I can't blame you for feeling that way. . . .'"

Members of the Mormon church are different from their fellow Christians in many ways. Belonging to their church means belonging to a community. And many of the customs of that community were designed to help them take care of each other in a hostile world.

Mormons are expected—not required—to give 10 percent of their income to the church. They are not the only Christians who do this, but it is more commonly practiced in the Mormon church than in most. They are not supposed to smoke or to drink alcohol, coffee, or tea. The church suggests that they keep a year's supply of food in storage in case of an emergency. There are many other guidelines for

Mormons like Gene and Maryanne Schmidt. That's the way Maryanne sees them—as guidelines.

"What I've had to do was just say

Portrait of America

John Yesco

what's important to me. What can I do that makes me happy and is still within the commandments that we have received. I've really had to look at myself and say, okay, I don't do this, I don't can ten million cans of fruit in the fall,

At the left are Maryanne and Gene Schmidt. The statue of Christ (above) is in the Mormon Temple in Salt Lake City.

21

that's great for those people who do. I personally keep a journal and a lot of people don't do that. I've had to say what is important to me and what do I want to do with my life."

One part of the Mormon church's effort to make its members self-sufficient can be seen at Welfare Square. Here, Mormons volunteer their labor to can and process food that will be

These two photographs show volunteers in Welfare Square.

given to church members in need.

Gene Schmidt went to work in the Welfare Square butcher shop when he suddenly lost his job. It could have been a very hard time for Gene and Maryanne.

"We just didn't know when he was going to get a job or whether or not the bills would be paid. . . . And having the church around really helped to put food on our table with some dignity."

The Mormon principles are charitable, practical . . . and sometimes hard to stick to. After all, as Gene Schmidt points out, he lives and works in a world that operates another way.

"As the world's standards of behavior seem to change over time, as the societal mores change, the church's standards remain the same. And as I see the standards changing, sometimes it's very difficult for me to be out in the world, Monday through Friday, in the working world."

A Tribe Is Reborn

"Well, one time, the Paiutes owned all this land, everything. When the federal government came to help my people, they put them on reservations. They gave them certain sections of land. And then they terminated our tribe in 1954. And then my tribe was left without any federal recognition. And they made a lot of promises to my people."

The Paiutes were once the richest tribe in the Utah region. Before the coming of the white men, they lived on the best land and had the most advanced way of life. When the settlers came, and especially after statehood, they lost most of that land. They

Against the background of a nineteenth-century photograph of Paiute Indians are two present-day Paiutes.

were pushed onto smaller and smaller reservations.

When the federal government dissolved the tribe—at least, as an officially recognized group—they gave pieces of land to individual members of the tribe. Now, the Paiutes would be expected to live as any other American citizens. But they had not been taught this new way of life. Among the things they had not been taught about were taxes.

"A lot of my tribal members lost their land through back taxes. They didn't understand about taxes and all that, and so they lost approximately fif-

teen thousand acres of land."

That is not all the Paiutes lost. Without a tribal home, they could not live according to the customs and rituals of their people.

Now, Congress has restored the Paiute reservation and given the Paiutes their tribal status back. But their old way of life must be rebuilt. And the Paiutes themselves must rebuild it.

"They've been kicked in the back so many times that it's hard for them to trust other people. And it's hard for them to get back into knowing who they really are."

It is hard, but the Paiutes are determined. Paiute leaders who are working toward that goal have begun to have powwows that bring the whole tribe together.

" . . . this powwow that the tribe is having is hopefully going to rejuvenate some pride in the younger people and teach our older people that, yeah, we want to learn."

The Paiutes are looking to their past. But they are using that past to give themselves and their children a future.

Utah's Resources: Mines and Minds

When the Mormons first came to Utah, they built a self-sufficient economy based on agriculture and handicrafts. What they needed, they raised or made. The railroad changed all that.

When it became possible to ship goods out to other parts of the country, the people of Utah started to specialize. They raised crops to sell. They dug into the earth for metals that would bring cash into the economy. Soon, the state was becoming dependent on mining. World War II changed all that.

Mining is still an important part of the Utah economy and so is agriculture. But now, government is the state's largest employer. And manufacturing is the largest area of

The state capitol building.

production.

Almost 22 percent of Utah's workers are employed by the federal, state, or local government. Many of them work in military installations or do research.

More than half of the value of goods produced in the state comes from manufacturing. The largest part of that—the production of primary metals—is tied in directly with the state's mining.

The primary metals industry smelts, refines, and rolls metals. The metal is then shipped to other factories—in Utah and other states—to be made into metal products. Much of the raw material comes from Utah's mines.

The second largest area of manufacturing is nonelectric machinery. Factories near Salt Lake City make office machinery and equipment for the construction and mining industries.

The manufacture of transportation equipment is also an important Utah industry. For the most part, this industry makes parts for aircraft of all kinds.

Two of Utah's industries include the precision manufacturing of aircraft parts (below) and the mining of hydrocarbons (inset).

Next to manufacturing in importance is mining. The riches under the land of Utah were responsible for bringing in the only big rush of population after the first settlement. That was more than a century ago. Today, the mines are still producing.

The most valuable mineral produced in Utah is copper. The state is second only to Arizona in the amount of copper it produces. Petroleum is second in value, followed by gold, iron ore, selenium, uranium, vadium, and zinc.

Utah also produces coal, more coal than most western states. But the riches of the land do not stop there. In just those places where farming has never thrived, the land gives up salt, silver, sand and gravel, and other minerals too numerous to mention. All of this comes from land that, once, no one wanted.

Important as mining and manufacturing are in Utah, agriculture is still strong. Farms cover about one-quarter of the state's land. Most of it is irrigated land, but a large part can also be farmed without irrigation.

As in most western states,

Courtesy of Utah Travel Council

cattle is the biggest farm product. And milk comes in second. But sheep are important, too. Utah is a leader in wool production. Most of the field crops in Utah are grown to feed livestock.

And of course, beautiful as Utah is, there are bound to be tourists. They bring in over $200 million a year.

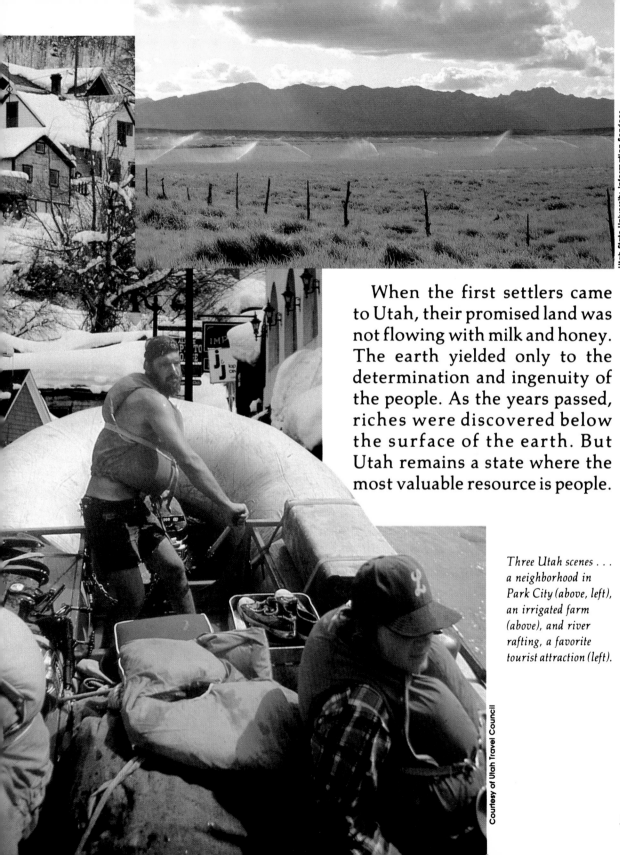

Utah State University, Information Services

When the first settlers came to Utah, their promised land was not flowing with milk and honey. The earth yielded only to the determination and ingenuity of the people. As the years passed, riches were discovered below the surface of the earth. But Utah remains a state where the most valuable resource is people.

Three Utah scenes . . . a neighborhood in Park City (above, left), an irrigated farm (above), and river rafting, a favorite tourist attraction (left).

Courtesy of Utah Travel Council

31

The Utah Arm

"When I was in intensive care—I guess it was just when I was coming out of surgery—I could feel it. It felt like it was just laying over my stomach, and it was just itching. And I couldn't—I tried to—I was going to scratch it—and I couldn't find it. And I remember saying, asking the nurse, 'Well, where's my arm?' And she goes, 'Well, you lost it in the accident,' you know. And I was going, 'Oh,' and I rolled back over and went back to sleep."

Shauna Bingham is eighteen years old. She's accepted the loss of her arm with courage and a sense of humor. She had to learn how to do a lot of things all over. It couldn't have been easy, but to hear Shauna tell it, it was.

"There was this one day I thought, 'Hey, I'm kind of hungry.' So I go in the kitchen. And I got out a can of soup. 'This looks good!' And I got the pans out and everything and I set it up on the counter, and I just stared at the can opener. And I thought, 'How am I going to do this?' It was so funny. So I called my mom up at work and I said, 'Well, I got something else for you. I can't open a can of soup.'"

As you might expect from listening to her, Shauna opened that soup. Everybody at her mom's office came up with suggestions and Shauna ended up sitting on the counter and pushing the handle of the can opener with her foot.

But even with that kind of cleverness and that willingness to try whatever might work, a lot of things were still difficult or impossible for Shauna. That's where Steve Jacobson comes in.

Steve Jacobson is an engineer who works at the University of Utah. He came up with a design for an artificial arm that he thought would work better than anything he's seen. When they said it couldn't be built, he built it. When no one would manufacture it, he started his own company. And he made the arm that Shauna Bingham now uses.

"They told me that I probably wouldn't be able to have one, because the whole top of my shoulder got crushed. . . . So I had no idea that I would be able to get an arm. So it was kind of fun, getting into it. It's hard to get used to, though, because—I don't know—nine months of it not being there and all of a sudden I've got one. I don't know what to do with it. It's weird."

It's also amazing. And, according to Steve Jacobson, it's what technology should be doing.

"Someone goes to an air show and they see a jet plane go screaming across the foreground and they think, 'Boy, look at that technology!' And they see the people land on the moon and they say, 'Boy, look at that technology!' . . . But the fact is, arms are more miraculous than either one of those things. They really are."

Below is Shauna Bingham being fitted with her new arm.

A Pioneer Culture

Utah is a young state in a young country. It is a place where all of life has been closely tied to surviving. And the character of Utah's art and culture reflect that.

Singing around the campfire and along the trail was one way that the early pioneers made their life gentler among the hardships. There were songs from home and songs about life on the trail. Out of that grew a tradition of choral music . . . and the Mormon Tabernacle Choir.

The Mormon Tabernacle Choir was formed to sing in the great tabernacle at Salt Lake City. It has developed a reputation for excellence that is worldwide. It has made records. It has toured. And it has always sung music that communicates some spiritual value to its listeners.

This is Maude Adams in the role of Peter Pan.

Portrait of America

At the left is a director of the Mormon Tabernacle Choir against the background of the choir. At the right is Cyrus Dallin working on one of his sculptures.

The writers of Utah have also come out of this pioneer tradition. Bernard De Voto was a critic and historian who had a unique appreciation for things American. His book *Across the Wide Missouri* won a Pulitzer Prize in 1947. His writing about Mark Twain was marked by an insight that came from his own experience of life in the Ameri- can West. He was one of the first to applaud what was truly Amer- ican in our literature instead of looking for an imitation of the classic literature of Europe.

One of Utah's finest writers is Wallace E. Stegner. He, too, writes history. Perhaps when you're as close to history as the people of Utah are, it's hard to

resist. But he also writes stories and novels with a strong sense of realism, works grounded in history and in the life of rural America. In 1972, he won the Pulitzer Prize for his novel *Angle of Repose.*

Much of the painting and sculpture of Utah has also been historical. There are, for example, the sculptures of Indians done by Cyrus Dallin and the monuments created by Brigham Young's grandson, Mahonri Young.

And one more Utah artist should be mentioned. At first glance, she doesn't seem to fit into the mold of realistic, historical, pioneer art. But Maude Adams, the great American actress, was a daughter of the West. She charmed audiences around the world with her honesty and her humor. She seemed born to play spirited, sometimes tomboyish heroines. And no one who ever saw her could forget her in her most famous role, a role she created—Peter Pan.

Along with her sense of history, the impressive realism, there is always room in Utah for a feeling of adventure.

Home on the Range

"You know, most people come to this country and they look at it and say, 'What in the world does a cow eat here?' I guess you'd have to live here for a while before you come to know it."

A lot of things have brought people west, to states like Utah. For some, it was the promise of gold and silver. For some, like the Mormons, it was the hope of a new life and freedom from persecution. To many, a century ago and still today, it is the lure of the West itself.

"When I was just maybe in high school, or maybe before, and I lived in the Smoky Mountains of North Carolina, I read all the Zane Grey books I could find. And I knew that someday I was going to go to the West. And someday I was going to have a little ranch in the West somewhere. And Utah happened to be the place where I could find one about—just about—what I wanted, that was run-down enough to where I could afford it."

Utah State University, Information Services

Against the background of Utah ranchland is rancher Cecil Garland.

John Yesco

Cecil Garland's childhood dreams of a western ranch came true in Utah. And if the land is so dry that it's hard to see what a cow could eat, Cecil doesn't mind. He and his family make it work for them. They also don't mind being miles away from anywhere.

"The question, I guess, that people ask most often who come out here is, 'How do you get along without a doctor? How do you get along without a supermarket? What do you do when you need to go for entertainment?' Well, the answer to all of these questions, of course, is ourselves. We've become, largely as we can, our own supermarket."

That's the kind of self-sufficiency you find in a lot of Utah. These people don't depend on themselves and their communities just because they have to. That's the way they like it. They like freedom and they have a pretty good sense of what freedom costs.

"I think the thing that we're losing, have a tendency to forget, in this country—that with freedom comes a great personal responsibility, the ability to determine for yourself that which is essentially correct. . . . And without that personal responsibility, that essential concern for welfare, not only of yourself, but of your neighbors and your country, then freedom is lost."

These two scenes—one in winter and one in summer—show the starkness of some of Utah's land.

The Future of a Young State

In the original colonies, one hundred and fifty years after the first settlement, the people were facing the problem of whether to declare their independence from Britain. In Utah, less than one hundred and fifty years after the first settlement, the people are facing the problems of the nuclear age.

That's quite a difference.

There is so much land in Utah that people can still decide about! Will it be preserved in its natural state for people to enjoy as a wilderness? Will it be used for more power plants, for agriculture, for mining? Utah is a state being formed. Compared to the older parts of this country, it is in its adolescence.

Bryce Canyon.

The Utah countryside.

And what about water? Like so many states in the West, Utah is short on water. How can the state provide for continued growth of industry and population without stripping the supply of this most valuable natural resource?

There is a different feeling about these choices than there was in the days when Massachusetts was making them, or New York or Pennsylvania. In the twentieth century, we have become very aware that there is a limit to what the land can give us.

And yet . . . the younger states, like Utah, want to grow up big and strong like their older brothers and sisters. And for many, growth means economic growth, industrial growth.

It's a difficult question. And it's one that Utah will have to face in the years to come. But there's one thing for certain. The twentieth century is an exciting time to be growing up.

Important Historical Events in Utah

1540 The first white man to visit the Utah area may have been the Spanish explorer Garcia L. de Cardenas.

1776 The Franciscan friars, Silvestre Velez de Escalante and Francisco Dominguez, explore the Utah region while looking for a route from New Mexico to California.

1811 The first Americans to visit the area are probably fur traders crossing over northern Utah.

1821 Mexico wins its independence from Spain and claims Utah.

1824 The well-known scout Jim Bridger finds the Great Salt Lake.

1826 The first American overland expedition to California is led by Jedediah Smith through Utah. He returns to Utah the following year.

1830 Many people now pass through Utah enroute from Santa Fe, New Mexico, to Los Angeles.

1832 The Uinta Basin trading post is built by Antoine Robidoux.

1843 The Salt Lake area is explored by Kit Carson and John C. Frémont.

1847 Brigham Young leads a group of Mormon pioneers to the Great Salt Lake. They begin to irrigate the valleys, making farming possible.

1848 Swarms of grasshoppers threaten to destroy the Mormons' crops. The "Mormon crickets" are stopped by flocks of seagulls from the Great Salt Lake. The United States gets Utah from Mexico in the Treaty of Guadalupe-Hidalgo.

1849 The Mormons organize the State of Deseret and make the capital Salt Lake City. They also aid other Mormons to come to Utah by setting up the Perpetual Emigrating Fund.

1850 The University of the State of Deseret is created. Congress organizes the Territory of Utah. The capital stays at Salt Lake City, and the governor is Brigham Young.

1853 Ute Indian chief Walker attacks Mormon settlements. The *Walker War* is fought over slavery among Indians and the invasion of white people onto Indian land.

1854 Chief Walker is persuaded to stop his attacks.

1857 President James Buchanan tries to gain control of Utah by removing Governor Brigham Young and installing his own governor. Buchanan sends federal troops to enforce his decision, and they are attacked by a group of Mormons and Indians in the *Mormon War.*

1858 Peace is made between the Mormons and the federal government.

1860 The Pony Express crosses through Utah.

1861 The first transcontinental telegraph service becomes operational in Salt Lake City, where lines from the east and west meet.

1862 Congress makes polygamy illegal and rejects the new constitution of the State of Deseret. Federal troops are again sent to Utah.

1863 Silver and lead are mined in Brigham Canyon.

1865   Ute chief Black Hawk leads attacks against Mormon settlers.

1869   The Union Pacific and Central Pacific railroads link up at Promontory, creating the first transcontinental railroad.

1887   The U.S. government passes a law allowing the government to seize church property from the Mormons for use by public schools.

1890   The Mormon church prohibits polygamy. The Utah public school system is established.

1896   Utah is admitted to the Union on January 4 as the 45th state. The capital is Salt Lake City, and the governor is Heber Wells.

1906   Surface-mining methods are introduced at Bingham Canyon, increasing the state's copper production.

1913   Strawberry River, a huge federal irrigation project, is completed.

1914   Bonneville Salt Flats becomes the site of auto racing.

1919   Zion National Park is created.

1928   Bryce Canyon National Park is created.

1952   The six-mile-long Duchesne Tunnel irrigation project is finished. Uranium is discovered near Moab.

1959   Utah becomes an important missile producing center.

1964   The Flaming Gorge Dam on the Green River is finished. The Glen Canyon Dam in Arizona creates Lake Powell.

1965   Canyon Lands National Park is created.

1966   Bridges over the Colorado River, the Dirty Devil River, and the White Canyon are all built within a six-mile radius.

1967   The Central Utah Project is begun to provide water for Utah's major growth centers.

1974   The federal government leases oil-shale land to private oil companies for millions of dollars.

Utah Almanac

Nickname. The Beehive State.

Capital. Salt Lake City.

State Bird. Seagull.

State Flower. Sego lily.

State Tree. Blue spruce.

State Motto. Industry.

State Song. Utah, We Love Thee.

State Abbreviations. Ut. (traditional); UT (postal).

Statehood. January 4, 1896, the 45th state.

Government. Congress: U.S. senators, 2; U.S. representatives, 3. **State Legislature:** senators, 29; representatives, 75. **Counties:** 29.

Area. 84,916 sq. mi. (219,931 sq. km.), 11th in size among the states.

Greatest Distances. north/south, 345 mi. (555 km.); east/west, 275 mi. (443 km.).

Elevation. Highest: Kings Point, 13,528 ft. (4,123 m). **Lowest:** 2,000 ft. (610 m).

Population. 1980 Census: 1,461,037 (38% increase over 1970). **Density:** 17 persons per sq. mi. (7 persons per sq. km.). **Distribution:** 84% urban, 16% rural. **1970 Census:** 1,059,273.

Economy. Agriculture: wheat, hay, apples, barley, beef cattle, milk, poultry. **Manufacturing:** electrical and electronic equipment, guided missiles and parts, primary metals, nonelectric machinery, transportation equipment. **Mining:** gemstones, gypsum, petroleum, copper, gold, coal, zinc, sand and gravel, uranium.

Places to Visit

Beehive House in Salt Lake City.

Bingham Canyon Copper Pit, near Salt Lake City.

Bonneville Speedway, near Wendover.

Golden Spike National Historic Site in Promontory.

Great Salt Lake, near Salt Lake City.

Monument Valley, southeastern Utah.

Indian Cliff Dwellings, near Blanding, Bluff, Kanab, Moab, Parowan, Price, Vernal.

Trolley Square in Salt Lake City.

Annual Events

Ute Tribal Bear Dance in Duchesne (April).

National Art Exhibit in Springville (April).

Strawberry Days Festival in Pleasant Grove (June).

All Tribes Indian Days in Bluff (June).

Festival of the American West in Logan (July-August).

Shakespearean Drama Festival in Cedar City (July-August).

Utah State Fair in Salt Lake City (September).

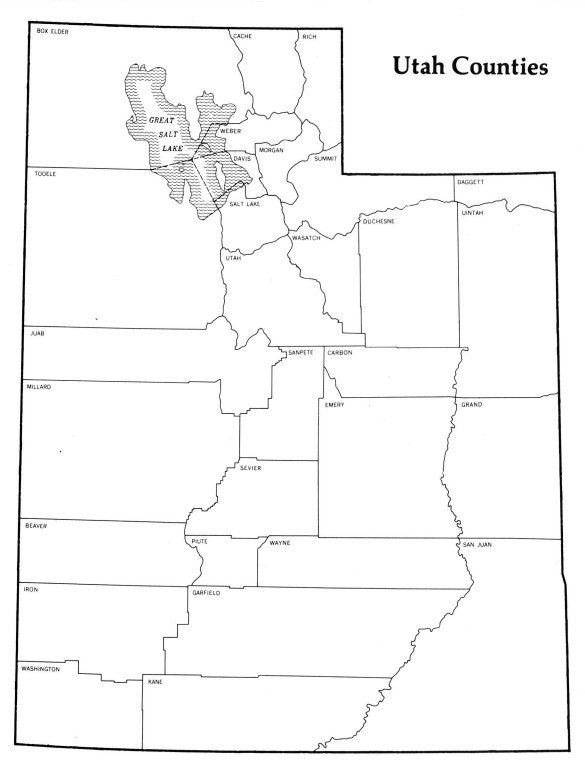

Utah Counties

BOX ELDER

CACHE

RICH

GREAT SALT LAKE

WEBER

MORGAN

DAVIS

SUMMIT

TOOELE

SALT LAKE

DAGGETT

UINTAH

DUCHESNE

WASATCH

UTAH

JUAB

SANPETE

CARBON

MILLARD

EMERY

GRAND

SEVIER

BEAVER

PIUTE

WAYNE

SAN JUAN

IRON

GARFIELD

WASHINGTON

KANE

INDEX